True S
Stories
Vol. 1

DEBRA GLASS

DEDICATION

For Jeddy, who ironically *believed* in me.

CONTENTS

ACKNOWLEDGMENTS

I would like to thank the following people who so generously shared their stories with me: Zak Abramson, Margaret Austin, Faye Axford, Cleo Coleman, Lee Freeman, Jean Ann Gifford, Dan Glenn, Benny Gooch, Gary Green, Lois Henderson, Bill Jarnigan, Bill Marthaler, Don McBrayer, Iva McClure, Bill McDonald, John L. McWilliams, Mary McWilliams, Debra Miller, Mary Nicely, Brad Nichols, Linda Quigley, Betty Rickard, Chris Robertson, John Vandiver, Beth Wallace, Susan Warren, and Marilyn Watson.

Cover art by Tricia "Pickyme" Schmitt

Back cover author photo by Mary Carton

PRISCILLA

Late fall has always held the reputation as the time when the partition between this world and the netherworld is at its most thin, when the dead are able to pass through and roam the earth.

On the campus of the University of North Alabama, fall is also a time to celebrate the return to school after the summer break, to the rush and whirl of college life, to the excitement of football games and parades.

But fall, it seems, is also the time of year that boasts the most encounters with one of the University of North Alabama's most active spirits.

UNA began as LaGrange College in 1830, the first state-chartered college in Alabama, and moved to its present site in downtown Florence, Alabama, in 1854. In 1872, it became the first state-supported teachers college south of the Ohio River, and one of the first institutions to offer a coeducational curriculum.

In 1911, Florence native, and Alabama Governor Emmet O'Neal, approved a state appropriation of $50,000 for the construction of the institution's first dormitory for women.

Just south of Wesleyan Hall, construction on the imposing, four-story, brick structure began. The dormitory was a magnificent structure, built on a terraced hill, to house 125 students, and included

1

a reception hall, lounge, offices, guest rooms, and also a workout room. The first floor contained the college cafeteria, and by the 1950s, a student center dubbed The Lion's Den which boasted televisions and a laundering facility.

In 1930, the massive brown brick dormitory with its soaring stone-trimmed tower, was dubbed O'Neal Hall in honor of the former governor.

Long after O'Neal Hall ceased to house students, it served as a commuter lounge and offices for UNA's sororities and fraternities.

During the 1980s, a North Alabama student, Robert Loften, found himself alone in O'Neal Hall, left to lock up the building after a fraternity meeting. Robert played football for UNA, and usually didn't mind being alone on campus long after everyone else had gone home.

As he started to close the side door to the building, a breeze rattled the gnarled tree limbs in the big oak between O'Neal and Lafayette Hall. A chill raced up Robert's neck, but he shook it off. Still, he couldn't rid himself of the sensation that he wasn't alone as he locked up the dark, lonely old building.

He grasped the knob and just as he was about to pull the door to, he heard a noise coming from inside O'Neal Hall. Robert peered into the dark side entrance. "Who's there?"

But no one responded. Thinking he'd watched one too many scary movies, he blew out the breath he'd been holding. The old hinges gave out an ominous creak as he started to close the door again.

Once more, a muffled sound drifted out of the shadows. Pulse rioting, he leaned in to listen. "Anybody there?" he called again. He snorted. One of the guys was probably playing a joke on him. They'd all have a big laugh about spooked he was tomorrow.

But when a plaintive sob echoed in the darkness, Robert's heart skipped a beat. Someone was still inside the building.

Goosebumps rippled over his skin as he pushed the door open wide. He squinted in the gloom before stepping back into the stairwell where steps descended into the blackness of the basement and reached up toward the shadowy upper stories.

Straining to listen, he realized the sound was coming from the second floor.

Warily, Robert ventured up the stairs. "Hello!" he called. "Who's up here?"

His mouth was dry as cotton as he reached the landing. Gripping the iron handrail, he started up the next set of steps. "Hello!" His voice echoed in the vacant stairwell.

A shard of moonlight sliced through the naked windows, illuminating a figure in the second floor hall near the old elevator shaft.

Riveted, Robert gaped.

This was no fraternity brother joke.

Clad in a gauzy, white nightgown, a barefoot young woman, with

3

long black hair, turned and stared back him. Tears streaked her cheeks. Her lips parted as if she might speak, but she emitted no sound. She reached out, her fingers extending in unspoken invitation.

A shiver crawled up Robert's spine.

The eerie knowledge possessed him that something wasn't right about this girl.

A soft glow surrounded her as if she were made of the moonlight itself. Everything about her deathly pale appearance seemed faded. Hazy.

A thousand thoughts raced through Robert's head. This girl was in trouble. She was lost. She was afraid. She'd been crying. He'd been about to lock her in the building! He had to help her. But just as he started to call out to her, she took a step toward him and a stark realization seized him. The moonlight shone *through* her.

A ghost!

Cold terror paralyzed him. He blinked, hoping it was a trick of the light, but she was still there, still holding out her hand to him as she floated toward him, slowly at first and then rushing at him, in a blast of icy air, with breakneck speed.

Somehow, he made his legs work. He whirled and bounded down the stairs, three and four at a time, stumbling as he lunged out the side door. Trembling uncontrollably, he yanked the door closed and managed to twist the key in the lock, before racing down the hill to his car.

Robert never locked O'Neal Hall up for the night alone after that. And when he recounted the tale to his friends, he was surprised to learn they'd already heard of the ghost of O'Neal Hall.

One of the first recorded sightings of the ghost, happened one night in the 1930s, when O'Neal Hall still served as a women's dormitory.

Several students, including Lea Timmons, a young coed who'd later become a much beloved professor at the university, congregated in the second story hallway to study. Around midnight, Ms. Timmons said a girl in a diaphanous white nightgown, with long flowing hair, stepped out of the elevator and glided down the hallway before disappearing into one of the dorm rooms.

Ms. Timmons and her dorm mates didn't recognize the girl, so they followed her. But when they arrived at the room, no one was inside.

She later learned sightings of the mysterious specter were frequent during the wee hours in O'Neal Hall.

Priscilla, as she became known to O'Neal's residents, possessed a tragic story.

She'd been one of the first inhabitants of O'Neal after the dormitory opened in the early twentieth century. Other students claimed she kept to herself, that she didn't have many friends.

Rumors abounded that she'd been involved in an unrequited love affair with one of her professors. Some gossiped that she'd become pregnant outside marriage. Those who knew her better, said Priscilla came from a strict home and that her parents put undue pressure on her to make perfect grades.

But everyone agreed on one thing. Priscilla was despondent during her tenure at Florence State Normal College.

One night in late October, dressed only in a white nightgown, Priscilla met an untimely end when she hanged herself in the elevator shaft of O'Neal Hall.

No one knows what her last thoughts were as she secured one end of a rope around the rigging in the elevator shaft and the other around her neck, nor the fear and sadness she must have felt as she hurtled into the darkness.

Her corpse was discovered the next morning, suspended from a creaking rope, slowly twisting in the elevator shaft.

Sadly, Priscilla hasn't found the peace she so desperately sought, even in death.

Countless O'Neal dormitory residents witnessed the sound of the lift rattling up the shaft and the old wooden elevator doors with their stained glass panels, opening onto the second floor. Sightings of an ethereal mist floating out of the otherwise empty elevator became commonplace. Others recounted watching in horror as that mist took the shape of a nightgown-clad, tearful woman who tearfully glided up and down the corridors of O'Neal Hall.

In the early 1980s, Frank, a university security guard, who worked the night shift, had an unexpected spooky encounter in the building.

Another guard had heard rumors that the rope with which Priscilla had hanged herself still dangled from the crossbeam over the elevator shaft in O'Neal Hall. Frank scoffed. He didn't believe in ghosts.

But bored, the pair decided to go an investigate the claims.

Since the power had long ago been turned off to the second and third stories, , their only source of light was the flashlights they carried on their utility belts.

They unlocked the desolate building, climbed the stairs to the second story, crept past the elevator doors where Priscilla's restless spirit had so often been seen, and then they ascended to the third floor.

Both men jolted when something shot out of one of the abandoned dorm rooms and sailed between their heads. When they realized their *assailant* was only a pigeon, they laughed and chided themselves for being silly.

Indeed, birds and squirrels had nested in the long forsaken third story, and Frank told himself the creatures probably accounted for many of the weird tales circulating around campus.

When they reached the ladder to the attic, the other guard stepped back. "You first," he said.

With a true skeptic's sneer, Frank stuck his flashlight in his pocket and scaled the ladder while the other guard followed close on his heels.

The floors creaked under their weight as they investigated the attic. Two arched windows in the front of the building allowed in light from the streetlamps outside.

"Here's the shaft," Frank said, dropping to his knees and shining his light into the opening.

The elevator had been boarded up for decades, but Frank could still smell the burnt stench of old machine oil. His light illuminated the stack of counter weights, the steel hoist cables—and a scrap of frayed rope.

His gaze flicked to the other guard who stared back, wide-eyed. "Reckon that's it?" he asked.

"Only one way to find out." Frank put down his flashlight and stretched out flat on the dusty attic floor. He reached blindly into the shaft, groping until his fingers came in contact with the hank of rope.

"Got it," he said as he began pulling the rope up, hand over hand. At first, the long stretch of rope came up effortlessly. But without warning, something—or someone—jerked back. Frank braced himself with one hand and struggled to pull up the heavy weight with the other.

"What's wrong?" the other guard asked.

"I don't know. It got heavy all of a sudden," Frank explained. "It must be caught on something."

The other guard kneeled on the floor to help.

Together, they tugged but when they did, the rope began to swing. Something that felt like the weight of a dead body thumped hard against the sides of the derelict elevator shaft.

But before they could let go of the rope, an electrical shock shot through their arms.

Stunned, the released the rope, clambered to their feet and raced each other to the ladder. They fled down and ran for the stairwell, bolting down the two flights and out the side door. The pair didn't stop their hasty escape until they crossed Pine Street and ran breathlessly into the chain link fence that enclosed the playground of the Kilby Laboratory School.

Exhausted, they reached out to lean against the fence and sparks flew from their hands.

Neither of them ever went inside O'Neal Hall again.

In the 1980s, the ominous, 1911, Gothic structure, with its soaring crenellated tower and high-ceilinged rooms, was torn down to make way for an enlarged student union building, named in honor of longtime university president, Robert Guillot. The demolition of O'Neal Hall was especially heartbreaking to those who enjoyed ghost hunting for Priscilla, for they feared the ghost would vanish along with the time-worn brown bricks and stone.

But it seems, Priscilla has found a new home on UNA's campus.

Chris Robertson, a university employee with offices in the Guillot Center, says that sometimes at night he has the feeling that he is not alone. He hears odd noises in the new building, particularly, what sounds like the rusty hinges of a door being opened—or a rope creaking under the weight of a lifeless body.

Female students feel as if they're not alone in the restrooms on the north end of the Guillot Center. Some have even reported glimpses of a ghostly figure reflected in the bathroom mirrors.

One night, in 2011, a group of sorority sisters were on the Haunted History of the Shoals Campus Ghost Walk Tour, and while the guide regaled them with the story of Priscilla, the elevator door opened in the empty student center. Moments later, the door on the front of the building swung open, stayed that way for a couple of minutes, and then closed.

When some of the young women on the tour night, who were also student workers in the Guillot Center, recounted the story to their colleagues of Priscilla's ghost stepping out to join the tour, the electricity in their office shut off, but didn't go out in any other room in the building. Incidentally, their office had been built over the site of the old elevator shaft.

Perhaps Priscilla was letting them know she still haunted the site of her tragic death.

Coeds who enjoy fellowship in the University Center today may very well be communing with the spirit of a student who lived—and died—on the campus of UNA over a century ago.

A PROPER TOMBSTONE

Everyone who lives in the Shoals knows and loves Trowbridge's Restaurant in historic, downtown Florence. Enjoying a double dip of ice cream in the 1918 establishment is a delightful respite from the hot humid Alabama summers.

Trowbridge's Restaurant in Downtown Florence

Entering Trowbridge's is like stepping back in time. With its old-fashioned lunch counter and familiar wait staff, the restaurant has retained a nostalgic atmosphere that bespeaks its early twentieth century beginnings.

While on his way to a dairy convention, Texas native, Paul Trowbridge, passed through Florence. He fell in love with the area, returned to Texas, packed up the family and opened the Trowbridge Creamery in 1918. Shortly afterward, he developed the recipe for orange pineapple ice cream.

Very little has changed in the family owned restaurant over the century.

Lunch patrons are always prepared to wait for a table to become available so they can enjoy hot dogs, homemade chili, or Trowbridge's specialty, fresh made chicken salad.

It is hard, therefore, to believe that such a busy, local favorite is home to a restless spirit—or two.

That's what long time employee, Betty Rickard, thought until she actually saw the ghost for herself.

Betty arrived early one morning to do the prep work for the restaurant and make the chicken salad to be served that day. None of the other employees had yet arrived and Betty stood by the table in the kitchen to prepare the things they would need for the day.

The restaurant quickly filled with the aroma of freshly chopped celery and delicious chicken. But as Betty worked, she caught a flash of movement out of the corner of her eye.

Startled, she whirled just in time to see a young man walk by, wearing a blue and white checked shirt.

He stopped and for a moment, their gazes connected. And then, just as suddenly as he had appeared, Betty watched him fade into thin air.

Most people would have been frightened. But not Betty. She'd heard the other employees talk in hushed voices about the mysterious ghost, but this was the first time she had caught a glimpse of him.

Later that day, she told the story to her co-workers, describing what she had seen.

Lois Henderson, who happened to be dining in Trowbridge's that day, listened intently to what Betty had to say.

A member of both the Daughters of the American Revolution and the Daughters of the Confederacy, she had done extensive research on historic Florence.

"I know who your ghost is," Mrs. Henderson told them. "It's Charles Daniel Stewart."

And she knew why he haunted the building.

Charles Daniel Stewart

Before the Civil War, the Stewart family, had owned a beautiful two story antebellum house, graced with soaring white columns, on that same location.

James W. and Pauline Bridewell Stewart moved to Florence from Kentucky in 1840. By 1850, Pauline wore widow's weeds, but she supported her family by taking in boarders.

During the Civil War, when the Federal Army marched into to Florence, they burned several of the downtown buildings, one of which was the Masonic lodge across from the Stewart home.

With all the able-bodied men away fighting the Civil War, the Stewart women, Pauline Bridewell Stewart and her daughter Ophelia

Stewart Smith, were left alone and undefended from the Northern aggressors but this did not dampen their own brand of heroism. When Colonel Florence Cornyn came to Florence, in 1863, with his band of "Destroying Angels," they set several of the downtown buildings on fire, one of which was the Masonic lodge across from the Stewart home, on the corner of Court and Tombigbee Streets.

Ophelia Stewart Smith

In 1863, Pauline Bridewell Stewart begged the commanding Federal officer of Cornyn's cavalry to let her go in the burning building so she could save the jewels of the order which were used in Masonic ceremonies.

The officer granted permission and Mrs. Stewart dashed into the burning building.

Because Masonic gatherings were never held on ground level floors, Mrs. Stewart knew she would have to fight the flames and smoke to rescue the jewels which were on the second story.

Her daughter watched in horror from Court Street, fearing that her mother would die in the fire.

But finally, Mrs. Stewart emerged unscathed with the jewels. The jewels were transported to Montgomery and finally returned to Florence after the war and are the same jewels of the order which are used today.

Florence M. Cornyn

Life must have been difficult for Mrs. Stewart. She had been forced to watch while Federal troops occupied her town and burned buildings at random. She had lost many of her possessions to Yankee looters.

But worst of all, she had watched her beloved son, Charles Daniel Stewart, don a gray uniform and ride off to battle carrying with him the stars and bars of the Confederacy.

The men, who had enlisted, assembled at Wesleyan University (which is now known as Wesleyan Hall and is a part of the University of North Alabama campus) and the Stewart boy was among them.

He was the first to ride out of Florence, brandishing the flag which had been handmade by the women of the city. As a color bearer, the young man led the Lauderdale Volunteers, vowing, "This flag will float wherever honor and danger shall demand it wave. If honor and victory are not inscribed upon its fold, this flag will never return to Florence."

It was not long before Charles saw action.

Charles headed the Florence Battalion in the first battle of Bull Run or Manassas as southerners referred to it. This was the first major battle and everyone wanted to be involved in it because it was believed that it would be the first, last, and only battle of the war. The South merely wanted to defend southern land only and had no intention of engaging in aggression. The Northern objective was to capture the capitol at Richmond and put an end to the secession. Most of the commanders had only had forty-five days training and some had never led large companies of men. They paraded through the streets of Washington joined by Congressmen and other Washington celebrities and their families with packed picnic baskets, expecting to see a colorful show.

The Confederates were quickly pushed a mile south to Henry Hill. It was here that Thomas J. Jackson led his Virginians to the top of the hill and sat still facing the onslaught of Federal soldiers. Seeing this, General Bee, attempting to inspire his retreating troops yelled, "Look there boys, there's General Jackson like a stone wall, rally around the Virginians boys." The name stuck and the legend of Stonewall Jackson was born.

The battle raged on for hours and finally the Union soldiers began to retreat. Chaos ensued when the fleeing soldiers ran headlong into the spectators while being chased by the Confederates.

Never again would the public look upon war as a good show.

At the head of the Lauderdale Volunteers, Company H., 4th Alabama Infantry, Charles was in the direct line of cannon and rifle fire. He was soon seriously wounded but bravely kept his promise to keep the flag from touching the ground and struggled to hold it up until another soldier could relieve him of his duties. This flag was carried by seven different bearers during the course of the war, all of whom were killed as a result of carrying it.

Miraculously, the flag was never captured by Union forces.

After the war, the flag made its way back to Florence where Pauline Stewart wore it as a bustle to keep the federals from taking it.

That very flag, although worn by war and time, is now displayed in the Pope's Tavern Museum in Florence.

During the Civil War, disease and infection killed more soldiers than bullets and the outlook was grim for the young ensign.

It was believed for many years that Charles Daniel Stewart's body had been buried with the others who perished at Manassas, but according to Lois Henderson's careful research, the boy languished for nearly a month at his home on Court Street before he died on August 16, 1861.

He was buried in Florence Cemetery with only a small handmade grave marker that bears the initials C.S.A., Confederate States of America or Confederate States Army.

The young man's heroism in the first battle of Bull Run was hardly recognized by such an improper stone. But the war was on and times were hard for Southerners. Perhaps the family intended to erect a more fitting monument to poor Charles but, unfortunately, it was never done.

After Mrs. Henderson told the history of the Stewart home where Trowbridge's now stands, it was concurred that their ghost was indeed Charles Daniel Stewart and that he was unable to rest because a proper stone had not been erected to his memory in the Florence Cemetery.

The employees of Trowbridge's thought it was fascinating to have their very own ghost.

The Stewart plot, Florence cemetery

That is, until a blue and white checked shirt was discovered the next day, hanging on a doorknob in the back of the restaurant.

All the employees asked those who had been at the restaurant the day before if they knew to whom the shirt belonged, but no one ever claimed it.

After closer examination, Betty told them, "That looks like the shirt I saw the ghost wearing."

The waitresses hastily returned the shirt to the doorknob. When they returned to work the next day, the shirt had vanished.

Over time, the mysterious presence was forgotten until one morning when Betty Rickard found herself alone in the restaurant again.

As she walked past the bathroom, she noticed a man standing at the sink, gazing at his reflection in the mirror. This was odd because no one was supposed to be in the restaurant.

Betty stopped and backed up just to verify what she had seen but the man was gone.

Other employees have also seen the transparent image of a young man in the rooms above the restaurant. When he is seen, he slowly fades.

Footsteps are often heard on the stairs but, upon investigation, no one is found.

Another employee, Beth Weaver, was working in the back of the restaurant one night and heard the unmistakable metal against metal grating of the slide bolt on the back door being locked. When she checked, the door had indeed been locked, something the employees never did until time to close the restaurant for the night.

When Beth told the others, Trowbridge's owner, Don Trowbridge, dismissed it as the ghost.

Another waitress heard her name being called by an unseen source, and on occasion, the cash register has been known to levitate.

One employee witnessed two large metal pans fly off the shelf and slam into the wall on the other side of the kitchen.

A floor in apartment above the restaurant had been tiled with pieces of broken marble tombstones. The current resident's first renovation included pulling up the makeshift tiles and disposing of them.

Charles Daniel Stewart was not the only Civil War hero to inhabit the Stewart home.

His brother, Jim Stewart, was one of the last remaining Confederate veterans in Florence up until the time of his death, in 1931.

Just two months before his fourteenth birthday, young Jim enlisted in Company F, Fourth Alabama Cavalry. He was doubtless, one of the youngest soldiers in Roddey's Cavalry.

Jim served as General Phillip Roddey's postman, and he was given the task to deliver dispatches and mail to the various units in the brigade. It was dangerous work, dodging the Federal encampments, and often, Jim would swim across the Tennessee River, carrying the mailbag in his teeth.

He was captured when he happened upon a house occupied by Federals, but due to his age, the Union officer dragged the young cavalry soldier home and told Pauline Stewart, "You had better get that uniform off your son, Madam, and keep him at home or he will be arrested and sent to prison."

But as soon as the Federals evacuated Florence, Jim Stewart returned to his former position as Roddey's mail courier, a job he held until the war's end in 1865.

Jim Stewart

Charles Daniel Stewart wasn't the only soldier to die in the house that stood on the site.

When Union General William Sherman occupied the town in November, 1863, many of his staff officers quartered in the Stewart home. Captain A. P. Hall, who'd been wounded during a skirmish in Greenhill, also died in the house.

Before Hall's death, he was visited several times by a prominent Florence physician, Dr. Hugh McVay. Hall gave McVay his boots who sold them to Mrs. Sample for $10.00. She gave them to her brother who was a Confederate soldier.

Dr. McVay certainly held sympathy for the Union cause. In his Official Records report, of January 23, 1864, Union Brigadier

General Grenville M. Dodge writes to Lieutenant Colonel Phillips in Athens: "Dr. McVay says a force from Bainbridge passed up the Waterville road on Wednesday night. They went 15 miles and were still going on. How many men do you want to go down and clean out this band of rebels, and how many can you take from your command?"

Dr. McVay was a frequent visitor of the Union Captain A. P. Hall, who convalesced under the care of Pauline Stewart and her daughter, Ophelia Smith, at their home on Court Street.

In 1863, Captain Hall, who was a member of the 7th Illinois Regiment commanded by Colonel Rowett, heard that several horses had been hidden about 14 miles out of Florence on Butler Creek. He took his men to confiscate the horses and encountered a group of Southern bushwhackers. A skirmish ensued and Hall was wounded. He was brought back to Florence and taken to the Stewart home where he was attended by General Sherman's medics. Upon examination, it was determined he would not survive.

The Stewart women nursed Hall until his death, about month later, and then had him buried in the Florence cemetery, where his body remained until it was disinterred, by order of the War Department, and removed to the National Cemetery at Corinth, Mississippi.

Lois Henderson worked to procure a fitting monument for Charles Daniel Stewart to commemorate his valiant efforts that would have been lost to the ages were it not for her love of local historical research. It was erected, with military honor and ceremony, at the grave site in 2001.

Curiously, the friendly waitresses at Trowbridge's—and sometimes, the customers—still hear from their ghost.

MOLLY

There was nothing unusual about this Saturday night. Most of the members of the Kappa Sigma Fraternity had already left the fraternity house near the campus of the University of North Alabama. It was late, but a few guys were still sitting around, talking and playing one last hand of cards before calling it a night.

"Have you seen my dog?" The clear, innocent voice of a child interrupted their conversation.

All the guys turned to the source of the voice, the hairs on the back of their necks standing on end.

They knew that this was no ordinary child.

There, standing in the doorway to the room, was the translucent apparition of a little blonde girl, dressed in a pastel gingham dress.

She seemed to be awaiting an answer, her ghostly gaze searching each young man's horrified face in earnest.

The fraternity brothers wasted no time in getting out of the house. And at least one of the Kappa Sigs present that evening, refused to ever set foot in the house again.

The little girl's name was Molly and she is probably the most renowned and most visible ghost in Florence, Alabama.

The UNA Off Campus Bookstore

According to the legend, sometime in the 1930s, her family rented the upstairs of the Edwards house at 472 North Court Street. It is now the University of North Alabama Off-Campus Bookstore.

The legends surrounding Molly are all tragic.

Some believe that shortly after Molly's eleventh birthday, she went out one morning to play, dressed in a lavender checked dress and white pinafore, with her hair neatly done up in blonde ringlets.

Her beloved pet dog met her at the door. But instead of running to greet her as he usually did, he bared his fangs and snarled. Foam oozed from his mouth.

"What's the matter, boy?" she asked, her ringlets bobbing as she approached the dog. "It's me, Molly."

She reached out to pet him, to reassure him. But instead of his usual tail-wagging greeting, he snapped, his canine teeth shredding the flesh of Molly's petite hand.

Ms. Lea Timmons, a former professor at UNA, had two theories. One was that Molly was a victim of rabies and died a tragic death in an upstairs bedroom in the house. However, in the 1880s, famed scientist, Louis Pasteur, developed a vaccine that successfully stopped the incubation period of rabies if the condition was discovered in time. By the early twentieth century, and American pathologist named Anna Wessels Williams developed a diagnostic procedure that could quickly detect the presence of rabies. Because of treatment techniques available at the time, it is unlikely that Molly died from the disease.

All the legends regarding Molly's death involve her dog. The other version, told by Ms. Timmons, asserted that Molly had been playing too near the street, with her beloved pet. The dog ran out in front of a passing car and in a tragic attempt to save him, Molly lunged in front of the car, was hit and killed.

In death, Molly remains as vivacious and playful as she had been in life. Sightings of her ghost have been frequent, both inside and on the grounds of the Edwards house.

Shortly after her death, a man saw her playing in the yard very near the street. Not knowing she had died, he called her parents and informed them that their daughter was in danger of being hit by a car.

He was astonished to learn Molly had passed away.

It seems that Molly doesn't know ghosts are only supposed to appear at night.

One bright autumn day, during a college homecoming parade in the 1950s, several people riding on the floats noticed a little girl waving to them from the upstairs balcony on the front of the house. They all returned her waves and after the parade, raved about the cute little girl on the balcony.

That is, until someone told them Molly's tragic story and they realized they had been waving to a ghost.

Since then, many have reported meeting a little girl dressed in a pastel dress with bouncing blonde ringlets. She always asks politely and intently if the passersby have seen her dog.

When the house was owned by the Kappa Sigma fraternity,

Molly would frequently open and close the doors to the upstairs balcony.

One Kappa Sig, Bill Marthaler, witnessed Molly's attempts to get attention. He and some fraternity brothers were playing cards upstairs when they heard footsteps on the stairs. They had already locked up for the night and were not expecting anyone so they all went to investigate.

To their horror, they discovered that every door leading to the outside, both upstairs and down, had been opened.

At night, the residents would be awakened in their rooms by the rattling of the doorknob and then they listened, in horror, to the squeaking of old hinges as their doors opened and closed one by one.

One unfortunate housemate claimed he awakened in the house only to discover Molly's ethereal presence, standing beside his bed.

Another Kappa Sig said he had turned off all the lights in the house and locked up, but as soon as he had crossed the street, the lights were all back on again.

Late one night, a young woman was driving past the Edwards house when a swirl of lavender mist darted across the street, right in front of her car. She screeched to a stop, fearing she had nearly hit the child.

And then she watched Molly vanish.

In the 1980s, the house was sold and was renovated for use as a bookstore. During the renovation, UNA professor, Don McBrayer, was house sitting while painters worked on the outside. He went to lock the door at the bottom of the stairs so that anyone who came in the house would have to come in through the side door.

Not long after he sat down to enjoy an Alabama football game, he saw something out of the corner of his eye and looked to see a pink mist floating up the stairs.

He asserted many times he'd been in the house and had heard the distinctive padding of little footsteps upstairs in the room where Molly died. He continues to have unexpected encounters with the little ghost to this day.

While working at a desk with two student employees, he saw a little girl was past and into another room. He asked if anyone else had seen the little girl. No one had. And upon investigation, he discovered no one in the room he was certain he had seen the child enter.

The employees at the Off-Campus Bookstore say there are strange drafts in the house, even when no doors or windows are open.

The room where Molly died is always cold, even when heated.

When the room served as a storage closet, a lock was placed on the outside of the door. The next day, the mechanism would not fit together properly and the door could not be locked. In fact, any attempts at locking the door have failed.

The staff also states that they have trouble with electronic equipment not working properly, and report hearing creaks and thuds, as if furniture is being moved, coming from the upstairs.

Some years back, a news team from Birmingham, Alabama, came to Florence to do a story on Molly. When they tried to light candles to take a spooky photograph, the candles would not stay lit, their flames almost immediately snuffed out by an unseen presence.

In 2003, Leigh Ann Gullett went on the Haunted History of the Shoals Ghost Walk Tour and brought along her digital camera. She took several photographs of the house but was not prepared for what she found when she loaded the photos onto her computer. There, distinctly standing in one of the downstairs windows, was Molly.

At that time, Michelle Eubanks worked as a reporter for the Times Daily Newspaper. When she saw the photo, she exclaimed, "That's Molly!" She recognized the little ghost from an encounter she'd had while working at the Off Campus Bookstore.

Michelle had gone upstairs, to the room where Molly died, to bring some T-shirts down for restocking. Molly's room always made Michelle nervous so she began talking as soon as she went in. "I'll be out of your way in just a minute, Molly. Don't worry about me. I'm just getting these shirts."

As soon as she began talking, the lights in the room began to flicker and then Molly appeared in the doorway. Stunned, Michelle stared. The fairly solid little spirit gazed up at her and smiled, but Michelle skirted out the door, narrowly passing Molly. Michelle sailed down the stairs and told the others what she had seen, but when they returned, Molly had vanished.

Michelle said the experience was not frightening—but it was definitely one she'd never forget.

Molly can still be seen coming out the front door and skipping across the front yard of the Edwards house.

Kyla Weir is still not convinced she had an encounter with a ghost. It seems Kyla, who, at age nine, was playing near the bookstore when a child in a lavender gingham dress approached her and asked her if she would help look for her dog. Kyla spent the entire afternoon helping Molly, even going to home to enlist the help of her father, but when they returned, Molly had simply vanished.

Sightings and encounters with Molly are frequent occurrences at the Off-Campus Bookstore. Perhaps if you're passing by, she just might ask you if you've seen her dog.

Leigh Ann's Image of Molly

THE FORKS OF CYPRESS

The man, who had driven Dowdy Road many times before, clutched the steering wheel tightly. A fog had crept up from Cypress Creek, covering the ground in ghost-like wisps, making it impossible to see on the pitch-dark Lauderdale County roads.

This place never failed to unnerve him because, although he couldn't see it, he knew it was there—the skeletal remains of The Forks of Cypress.

A chill swept over him despite the humid Alabama heat.

Even in the daylight, the columns, all that was left of what was once a grand plantation home looked ominous, lonely.

The man slowed the car even more, wondering what life must have been like on the plantation nearly two centuries ago.

And that's when he heard it.

The pounding of horses' hooves thundering past mingled with the din of rowdy cheers.

The man's breath froze in his chest. His foot slipped from the accelerator as he tried but in vain to peer through the fog. Could he be mistaken or did he hear what sounded like a horse race?

But it couldn't have been. There were hardly any houses way out here, much less a horse track.

Baffled, he drove home and told his wife what he had heard.

"That's funny," she said. "The man who built the Forks used to have a horse track up there just north of the old family cemetery."

In the early 1800s, Irish immigrant, James Jackson, came with his friend, Andrew Jackson, to Lauderdale County. Though they weren't related, both Jacksons stemmed from the same county in Ireland. Andrew Jackson had fallen in love with the area when he'd marched his troops through on the way to fight the Battle of New Orleans.

James Jackson

The Shoals area originally belonged to the Chickasaws, who ceded the land to the federal government in the early nineteenth century.

Andrew Jackson, John Coffee, James Jackson, Judge John McKinley, and others formed the Cypress Land Company and, in 1818, hired Italian engineer, Ferdinand Sannoner to survey the area.

Sannoner was given the honor to name the town, and he chose Florence, after his hometown in Italy.

The city of Florence was established March 12, 1818.

James Jackson had spotted the rise of a hill near where Cypress Creek forked and he told Old Hickory that he intended to build his home there. James moved his family to Florence from Nashville and began construction in 1820, on his plantation home.

A stone cutter traveled from England to build the foundation which came from the limestone along the creek banks. Almost all the materials that went into the house were made at The Forks. It was a grand house with pristine white Poplar siding set off by green shutters.

The most unique feature, however, was the twenty-four Ionic columns that encircled the entire house, making The Forks look like a Greek temple nestled in the wilds of frontier Alabama.

The Forks of Cypress

Here Jackson spent his life running his plantation and raising thoroughbred horses, including Glencoe and Peytona. One can only imagine the gatherings at The Forks to watch the horses run the track. Jackson's watch, which he used to time his prized horses, is on display at Pope's Tavern museum.

Jackson's Prize Thoroughbred, Glencoe

Just east of the house, and secluded in the woods, the Jacksons chose a place for the family cemetery. A stone wall stretches around the weathered tombstones of James and Sally Jackson and several other family members. Some of the slaves were buried outside the wall, their graves now secreted by the woods.

James Jackson died in 1840, from complications due to an illness which was possibly malaria. A tall and fitting monument stands over his grave. At the base, there is a hole in the ground that has to be continually filled in.

The Civil War added to the anguish of the Jackson family. Relatives, John Kirkman and James Kirkman, both casualties of the war, sleep in the cemetery.

But there is at least one member of the Jackson family who doesn't rest.

Not long ago, a man was visiting the cemetery on a bright autumn afternoon, when a young man came riding up on horseback. The young man was friendly, introducing himself as Andrew, and the two started a conversation.

Young Andrew spoke of being home on leave from the war, and

of his parents who had built the house over on the hill.

Jackson Family Cemetery

The more he talked, the more the man realized that Andrew was talking about James and Sally Jackson and the war he referred to was the Civil War. He thought it a little odd but with so many people who were now a part of Civil War re-enactments, he thought he'd just come across a man who was a little too enthusiastic about his role.

Until Andrew shook hands with him and then horse and rider both vanished.

Sarah "Sally" Moore Jackson

The Forks must have been a happy place. It seems that all of the ghosts there are benign spirits, merely acting out events in their day to day lives.

When the house was still standing, historian, Faye Axford, spent several nights there in order to research the house. Although, her first night in the mansion unnerved her a bit when her bedroom door opened and closed, seemingly of its own accord, she found at least one spirit at The Forks to be quite helpful.

In the haste of getting ready to go one morning, she dropped some items on the floor. Since no one was going to be in the house that day, she decided she would just clean them up later.

But when she arrived back at The Forks later that day, her things had already been picked up and placed neatly together.

Could this be one of The Forks' many servants still acting out her day to day chores?

The Stone Cutter's Signature is the Curlicue on the Bottom Step

The ghost, it seemed, liked Mrs. Axford. When she returned to The Forks to continue her research, Mr. Dowdy, who served as the caretaker at the time, had put her suitcase in a different bedroom than the one to which she was accustomed.

She informed Mr. Dowdy that she'd already made friends with the ghost on the left side of the house, and as if to confirm Mrs. Axford's statement, the lid of a candy dish levitated off the dish, floated in mid-air for several seconds and then shattered.

Needless to say, Mrs. Axford slept in the bedroom on the left that night.

Tragically, the mansion burned in 1966, after being struck by lightning. Nothing but the columns survived the flames. They still stand today as a wistful reminder, the ghost of what was once a beautiful and magnificent plantation home.

The plantation ruins are on private property, however, wonderful and informative historical tours of the site and cemetery, sponsored by the Florence Lauderdale Tourism Department, are given annually.

GHOST BRIDGE

Jackson Ford Bridge on Lauderdale County Road 282, was built in 1912. The Pratt through truss structure was made out of steel with a wooden, one lane deck. It was a little over 300 feet long and only 11 feet wide.

The bridge spanned Cypress Creek in the vicinity of the Forks of

Cypress for just shy of a century before it was closed in 1996. In the early twentieth century, it served as a major connector between Savannah Highway and Florence.

No one is certain when the Jackson Ford Bridge became known as Ghost Bridge. Some believe the nickname was derived from the ghostly mist rising from Cypress Creek.

Just before the bridge closed, those brave enough to drive across were treated to the ominous creaking of the old wood and steel structure. And many a county school driver education student enjoyed navigating the narrow bridge for a thrill.

In the 1970s and 80s, the location garnered a reputation as a teen hangout, and many mischievous pranks were played on unsuspecting drivers.

Tall tales abound about the eerie crossing, but hardly any of them can be substantiated. Some alleged the bridge to be the site of slave hangings, but since the bridge wasn't constructed until nearly a half century after the Emancipation Proclamation, this theory is unquestionably false. Reports of murders and suicides are also, more than likely, made up.

After the road was closed in the 1990s, vandals littered the area and damaged the structure.

However, there's one story about the site that has its basis in historical fact.

Several visitors to the bridge at night have witnessed a mysterious green light—or swamp light—floating about waist high on the creek banks and in the woods near the crossing.

Long before the bridge was built, in October, 1864, Confederate Colonel, C. R. Barteau, had been driven from Factory Hill, a cotton mill village on Waterloo Road. Fearing for the safety of the Jackson family, Lieutenant Colonel George H. Morton dispatched the second Tennessee army to guard the ford near Ghost Bridge.

Morton posted lines and discovered he had been cut off by Union General Rousseau's cavalry brigade.

With bugles sounding, Lieutenant Colonel Morton led his men on a courageous charge head on into the Federal brigade. The

Yankees were completely surprised in a hand to hand combat attack that would later be considered one of the bloodiest skirmishes of the Civil War.

The Forks of Cypress was saved.

Colonel CR Barteau, CSA

Perhaps the lonely spirit who carries a lantern through the secluded wooded area is the ghost of one of the casualties of this skirmish, still searching for his dead and wounded compatriots.

Sadly, due to liability issues, Ghost Bridge was demolished and scrapped in 2013, despite valiant efforts to save it as a walking park.

The area is privately owned and trespassers are unwelcome. However, the dead most assuredly still wander the woods in the vicinity of the Forks of Cypress and the former Ghost Bridge.

MINNIE MA

In 1962, there was little that could be done for those who had been stricken with cancer.

Minnie Tucker was dying of the disease, awaiting the Reaper, in her 1876 home on Enterprise Street in Florence. She had been born in this house and she knew that soon, she would die here.

Angry that her body had betrayed her with disease, she lashed out at those closest to her, especially her husband, Grady.

She became convinced that he was trying to poison her, although he had no such intention, and she made terrifying threats which the family dismissed as the chatterings of a very sick woman.

"I'll come back for you, Grady Tucker," Minnie rasped, her gnarled finger pointed at him with accusation. "I'll come back as an animal after I die. And I swear I will claw your eyes out."

Minnie kept her macabre promise.

The family had just returned from Minnie's funeral when they heard a strange noise at the back door.

Upon investigation, they found a dark gray cat, howling and pawing at the door, its flashing emerald eyes filled with intent to gain entrance to the house.

For days, the cat lingered on the doorstep just waiting for its chance.

Grady began to wonder if Minnie had kept her word.

And then one day, when Grady's daughter opened the door to go outside, the cat seized its chance, darted into the house, and lunged at Grady.

Benny, Minnie's grandson, was a child then, but he remembers the events that followed with striking clarity.

Benny and his father rescued Grady from the cat and drove it across town where they turned it loose. Neither of them spoke about what they both had on their minds--Minnie's promise.

When they returned home, Benny's mother met them at the front door. "I thought you took that cat off."

"We did."

"Well, it's back," said Mrs. Gooch. "It's clawing at the back door again."

Benny and his father did not even venture to guess how the cat had beaten them back home.

But Minnie's promise was enough evidence for Grady.

He packed his bags and as he left, the cat hissed and growled at him, its back arched, its gray tail puffed and standing straight on end.

By this time, the family was beginning to suspect that this was no ordinary cat.

Benny's father trapped the cat and, once more, they loaded it into their car. This time, they drove it all the way to Savannah, Tennessee.

After they dropped the cat off on the side of the road, they spent the night at a campground and then returned to Florence the next day.

Both Benny and his father breathed a sigh of relief. The cat was some sixty miles away and would not be bothering them anymore.

But when they returned home, the cat sat on the back step, awaiting them.

Exasperated, Benny's father did the only thing he could do. He and Benny seized the cat, put it in the car and drove to Florence Cemetery where Minnie Tucker's body lay buried.

They turned the cat loose on the fresh grave.

"Minnie Ma," he told the cat, "If this is you, don't come back and give us any more problems."

The cat never returned.

But Minnie Tucker did.

This time, in the form of a ghost.

The family had moved next door and kept the Tucker home, on Enterprise Street, vacant, with the exception of a phone.

Late one summer night, the phone began to ring. Benny's father didn't know anybody who would call so late, so he covered his head with a pillow and tried to go back to sleep.

But the phone kept ringing. It rang for thirty minutes.

Benny remembers being awakened by his father and told he had to go with him to answer the phone. His father didn't like going into the Tucker house alone.

They unlocked the house and went inside and suddenly, the phone stopped ringing.

"Good. Let's go back home and go back to bed," Benny's father said.

They walked out of the dark house and onto the porch. But as they turned the lock and pulled the door closed, something pulled back.

"Let me out..." The voice was but an eerie whispered breath.

Benny said that his father dashed back to his house and had locked the door before Benny could get in. He had to stand and beat on the door before his father would open it and let him inside.

A few years later, the family moved back into the Tucker house. One day as they were leaving to go on vacation, Benny's father jokingly said, "Minnie Ma, you keep an eye on the house for us."

Suddenly, the curtains in the front window blew back, as if pulled by someone, and the whole family saw Minnie standing there, watching them leave.

Often, when the family was in the house, they would see someone dressed in brown walk by out of the corner of their eye. Unexplainable cold breezes wafted past them, even on sweltering summer days.

When visitors came to the house, they always slept in the room the family chose not to use—Minnie's room.

One night, while sleeping in Minnie's room, their cousin Robert was awakened by the feeling that he was not alone.

There, sitting in a rocking chair, was an old woman, and she was looking at him and smiling.

Robert went to Benny's father's room and shook him awake. "You're going to have to take me somewhere else," he said.

"Why?" asked Benny's father, although he very well knew the reason.

Robert described the old woman.

"That's just Minnie Ma. She won't hurt you."

But Robert refused to sleep in the house, much less in the room, and he demanded to be taken to a relative's house that night.

Minnie is not as active as she once was, but occasionally, the family still sees that flash of someone in brown out of the corner of their eye.

They know it's just Minnie Tucker, watching over her home and family.

THE WINSTON HOME

Judith Winston gazed out the window at the ominous yellow sky. Thunder rumbled in the distance and Judith closed her eyes against the terrible memories that sound evoked.

Only ten short years ago, the storm of cannon fire had resounded in Tuscumbia from as far away as Corinth, Mississippi. Except then, the skies had not been dark and the winds had been still.

Another boom of thunder shook the grand house to its foundation.

The sound conjured up dread in the pit of Judith Winston's stomach. Dread that the Yankees would return, take everything she and her family had worked for, and burn her beloved Georgian style home.

But this time it wasn't the Yankees.

It was the wrath of God.

Those war years, however, had hardened Judith and she was not about to let anyone, not even God, take her home.

Snatching her full black skirt up in one hand, she dashed up the gracefully curving staircase, breathless by the time she reached the attic. Oblivious to warnings from her sons to take cover, she hurried up the crude attic stairway and flung back the door that led up to the roof.

From here, she could view the entirety of the vast Winston plantation.

Judith Winston

And she could see the large black cloud, salient against the stormy sky, rending a path straight for Tuscumbia.

Wind whipped through her skirts and tore her graying hair from its chignon but Judith stood fast, defying the storm to come any nearer.

Suddenly, rain pelted her. Hail ricocheted off the tin roof. The roaring funnel of wind was fast approaching.

With one hand, Judith shielded herself from the punishing hail and with the other, she tried, but in vain, to control her multitude of skirts so she could navigate the narrow attic stairs.

The tornado was advancing much more quickly than she had anticipated.

Hanging onto the ladder-like stairs, she tried with all her might to pull the door to the roof shut.

"Mother, hurry!" Judith's sons called to her over the roar of the deafening wind.

Muttering an uncharacteristic—and quite unladylike—oath, Judith gave up and left the door open.

Tripping on her skirts, she hurtled down the steep stairs. Her son reached and his fingers grazed hers, but before he could assist her, a blast of wind peeled the roof away. She gaped up at the black sky just as the heavy truss beams and stairs plummeted down, crushing Judith Winston under the debris.

Her sons quickly rescued her from beneath the rubble and carried her to the front bedroom on the east side of the house.

However, it was too late.

Judith Winston died from the injuries she sustained moments later on that fateful day, November 22, 1874.

But Mrs. Winston, it seems, has not left her beloved home.

The Winston Home in 1939, After Years of Neglect

The house stood vacant for the earlier part of the twentieth century before being purchased by the city of Tuscumbia in 1948, for use as Deshler School. The Winston home housed many classes, and during that time, students, teachers, and custodians alike, began to notice strange things.

Doors would open and close. Strange drafts circulated through the house, even when the doors and windows were closed. Things would be mysteriously moved when no one had been in the house.

And sometimes, students claimed to have seen a woman standing at the window in the upstairs bedroom where Judith Winston died.

In 1981, after many years of neglect, Tuscumbians realized what a treasure they possessed and a community-wide effort was made to restore the house.

Now, the home is available for teas, weddings, receptions, and other functions.

But the inexplicable happenings still occur.

At night, lights appear in the house when it is vacant. Sometimes, floating candle light can be seen coming from the cellar where there were once passageways that led to underground caves.

Mary McWilliams, the curator of the Winston Home, asserts

candles will not burn in the Green Room, the room in which Judith Winston died. Once she was decorating for the holidays with battery operated candles. Even those candles refused to burn in that particular bedroom.

Thinking the batteries were dead, Mrs. McWilliams started downstairs with the candles to replace the batteries and, suddenly, all the candles lit up in her arms.

When an antique dresser was donated to the house, Mrs. McWilliams asked some of the Deshler football players to move it into the Green Room for her. As she was showing them where to put it, a cold breeze wafted around her and she had the feeling of someone standing behind her.

When she whirled to see who'd brushed by her, no one was there.

Those, who've used the home for functions, have reported doors opening and closing, various objects being moved to different places, and footsteps from an unseen entity traversing the hardwood floors and the stairs.

Mrs. McWilliams claims that Mrs. Winston's ghost is especially particular when there is to be a wedding in the house.

One time, as a woman was arranging seating for her daughter's wedding, all the chairs she'd set up began to rattle and would not stop. Terrified, the woman left and telephoned Mrs. McWilliams.

Mrs. McWilliams explained to the distraught mother that Mrs. Winston only wanted to be invited to the wedding.

When the lady returned to the house to continue preparations for the wedding, she stood at the front door and issued an oral invitation to Mrs. Winston. The chair rattling promptly stopped.

Sometimes, it seems as if Mrs. Winston is melancholy. The walls in the downstairs entry hall *weep* when there is the threat of an impending storm.

The Winston Home Today

Mrs. Winston must still love her beautiful home. She remains, in death, a genteel woman, possessing a gracious air of true Southern hospitality.

She only requests that she be allowed to take her rightful place as hostess.

THE HEADLESS GHOST OF TUCKER HOLLOW

As Roy Weston crossed the Waterloo bridge in his new 50s model truck, he honked his horn so his friend Ben Lee would know he was near.

Blowing the horn had become a custom with Weston and Lee, and now they did it on every hunting trip.

Roy found the parking spot they had picked out beforehand and chuckled when he saw he had beaten his friend to the meeting spot.

He stepped out into the chilly darkness and lit his lantern, relieved when a comforting glow brightened the area.

After gathering the rest of his gear, he opened the cages in the back of the truck and let his two coon dogs out.

After scratching each one in turn behind the ears, he chuckled again. "We beat ol' Ben here. He's gonna be right mad."

The dogs seemed to sense Roy's glee. They darted around the truck, sniffing the dry leaves which blanketed the ground.

"C'mon boys," Roy called to them as he started the long trek through Tucker Hollow.

But instead of running ahead as they usually did, the dogs stayed close to his feet, nearly causing him to trip.

He looked up at the nearly full moon, thankful for the light it shed. The woods were thick here and it was still pretty dark but Roy knew this Hollow like the back of his hand. He could have walked it even without a lantern. Still, the moonlight made it much easier. Especially with these dogs acting like they were.

While he walked, he liked to ponder what Tucker Hollow had been like in the 1860s. A Civil War skirmish had even been fought here. And Roy remembered the tales the old folks in Waterloo used to tell about hearing the cannon fire from as far away as the battle of Shiloh.

Occasionally, he stopped to listen for Ben's footsteps crunching in the leaves. During the fall, he could easily hear him coming from a mile away.

But he couldn't hear anything over the annoying whimpering of his dogs.

Roy finally arrived at the meeting place. He sank onto an old stump and put his gun and lantern down.

Both seasoned hunting dogs continued uncharacteristically pressing their bodies against Roy's legs. He tried to shoo them away but they would not be budged.

One snarled and growled, his gaze trained on the shadowy woods.

"What is the matter with you two?" Roy demanded, their odd behavior making him increasingly angrier.

He shook his head, pulled some rolling papers and his tobacco out of his pocket, and rolled his own cigarette.

Just as he was about to light it, he heard the sound of footsteps rustling through the leaves.

Roy peered into the darkness and spotted a figure headed his way. "Ben, looks like I beat you here," he said, "Think it might rain?"

But no answer came from the approaching figure.

Roy's dogs cowered against his legs even more.

"How was your walk up here?" Roy asked.

Still, there was no answer.

Roy snorted. Ben was really mad at him for beating him to the meeting spot! But that shouldn't give him cause to act like this.

And then Roy noticed something unusual. Ben had not brought his dogs.

"Why didn't you bring your dogs?"

No answer.

The figure continued to plod through the dead leaves, coming closer and closer.

Roy struck a match to light his cigarette. The light from the flame illuminated the most horrific thing he had ever seen in his life.

It was a man, standing merely a yard away—a man without a head.

Stunned, Roy dropped the match and groped for his gun and lantern. He curled his fingers around the gun. "Ben, if you're there, you better speak."

Still, there was no response.

"Ben, I'm gonna blow you to pieces if you don't speak to me."

Roy cocked his gun but the figure came closer, its heavy footsteps lumbering through the leaves.

Shaking uncontrollably, Roy aimed at the figure and pulled the trigger, the shot resounding through the whole hollow.

He'd hit whatever it was.

Grabbing his lantern, he held it high and searched for what he'd shot. Perhaps it was a bear.

But there was nothing.

Still shaking, Roy gathered up his things and all but ran down the hillside out of the hollow, his dogs close on his heels.

On the way, he ran into Ben.

"Roy, what in the world were you shooting at?" Ben asked.

Roy glanced over his shoulder into the darkness. Ben would never believe him if he told him.

"Oh, nothing," he replied. "Why don't we hunt someplace else tonight?"

Roy Weston never liked to hunt in Tucker Hollow after that incident, but he did enjoy telling the tale of the headless man to his grandchildren for many years afterward.

PARTHENIA

James Sample was one of the earliest settlers and wealthiest merchants in Florence, Alabama. In 1818, he opened a store on Court Street, and later, he owned and operated the first brickyard in town.

The brickyard was located near where the University of North Alabama president's home now stands. Sample employed hired slaves and also had a number of indentured servants who worked as brick masons.

Sample had his pick of any of the Florence belles and had narrowed his marriage prospects down to two of the most beautiful women in town. Their names were Susan and Parthenia McVay. They were sisters and daughters of a prominent Alabama politician, Hugh McVay. He served in the Alabama House of Representatives as well as the State Senate, and in 1837, he served a short term as governor of Alabama. He also had a large acreage plantation on Mars Hill Road near the King Spring Park area. In the 1970s, logs from the rustic three room plantation house were used to build a replica of W.C. Handy's birthplace on College Street.

James Sample married Parthenia July 1, 1819, and in 1826, built Wakefield, the first brick residence in Florence, for her as a wedding gift. The plans Sample used to build his magnificent home were the exact same plans used to build the original Wakefield—the birthplace of George Washington.

Florence's Wakefield is the only surviving replica of the Washington home.

Wakefield, 450 N Court Street, Florence

During her marriage to James, Parthenia gave birth to six children. She died, at the young age of thirty-two, presumably from complications during childbirth, on August 18, 1834.

James returned from the funeral and immediately remarried—his second choice—Susan McVay.

It only made sense to James Sample to marry his sister-in-law. What better stepmother for his five children than their aunt?

Not long after James moved his new bride in, strange things began to happen at the 450 North Court Street home in Florence.

Doors would open and shut of their own accord. The family noticed cold spots and drafts in the house, even in the midst of sweltering Alabama summers.

The floorboards creaked under unseen footsteps.

Unearthly noises rose from the dark, dank cellar.

Parthenia was clearly not happy that her own sister had taken, not only her home, but her husband and children as well.

It is not difficult to imagine how uneasy the newlyweds must have felt knowing that an unhappy spirit watched their every move, never letting them forget that Wakefield was hers.

At Susan's insistence, James sold Wakefield and the Sample family moved to a plantation in Pontotoc, Mississippi.

Despite Parthenia's ghostly presence, Wakefield came to be known as the essence of Southern charm and enlightened thinking.

The house was bought in the 1860s by Dr. W. H. Mitchell who served as the pastor of the First Presbyterian Church in Florence.

Rev. WH Mitchell

During this time, many prominent people visited Wakefield. The great southern orator and staunch secessionist, William L. Yancey, was among many famous guests who enjoyed Wakefield's hospitality.

And while Dr. Mitchell was in Federal prison for publicly praying for the success of the Confederacy, Union troops occupied the house, forcing the Mitchell family to live in the basement.

Parthenia must have loved her beautiful home, with its handsome crow-step gables and Doric columns, because although the Samples are long gone, she still continues to inhabit its high-ceilinged rooms.

Rev. WH Mitchell and his Family

Wakefield was home to photographer Dan Glenn for many years and Parthenia apparently liked the Glenn family, especially Mrs. Glenn who shared Parthenia's love for the beautiful antebellum home.

She rarely frightened the Glenns, but on occasion, they would hear the ancient floorboards groan as their invisible resident traversed the house.

Parthenia seems happy with the present owner, as well. Perhaps she is pleased with the careful work that has gone on in Wakefield to restore both the house and the gardens to their original Federal style splendor.

One evening, Parthenia left her calling card when the owner returned home to find every door in the house closed.

And once, during the renovation, the hot water faucet mysteriously turned on full blast.

Ghostly sounds are regularly heard coming from the cellar where perhaps, Parthenia still remains as Wakefield's mistress, overseeing the long dead staff reenacting their duties.

Although her presence doesn't bother the new owner, his dogs tell a different story. They refuse to enter the downstairs room where Parthenia died.

It is almost as if life at Wakefield has made a historical imprint on time. As if long deceased occupants continue the tradition of Southern gentility and hospitality.

Some nights, faded figures in antebellum dress can be seen entering the foyer, passing their coats to servants, and greeting the Sample family.

Perhaps, in death, Parthenia is merely enacting scenes from the life of which she was so youthfully robbed.

She is buried in the McVay family cemetery, amidst the tall, ancient cedars—but her spirit still dwells within the walls of Wakefield.

An Image Captured on the Haunted History of the Shoals Ghost Walk of What Appears to be a Woman in Antebellum Dress on the Porch

Belle Johnston portraying Parthenia on the 2014 Haunted History of the Shoals Ghost Walk Tour

A GHOST IN THE O'NEAL HOME

Nancy Johnston lay awake, a thousand thoughts racing through her mind.

The foremost was gratitude that her family and her cat had miraculously survived the awful fire that had destroyed their home. She was glad her house on Oakview Circle would soon be rebuilt and she was very appreciative to the Roulhac family who had so graciously allowed her family to use the historic Governor Edward Asbury O'Neal home as their temporary residence.

The upstairs portion of the O'Neal home was closed off by a door at the top of the stairs and the Johnstons lived only in the spacious downstairs rooms of the house.

Perhaps that is why Nancy was alarmed, one night, when she heard a noise in the room above her.

While everyone else in the house slept, Nancy sat, reading a book. A scraping sound came from the upstairs floor, as if someone were dragging a heavy piece of furniture across the heart of pine floors.

Nancy got up and checked on her sleeping family, but they were all still asleep. Uncertain of what she'd heard, she attributed the noise to the age of the house and then she, too, drifted off to sleep.

When the housekeeper, Cleo Coleman, arrived the next day with the key that unlocked the doorway between the first and second stories, Nancy described the awful noise and the two went upstairs to investigate.

Cleo unlocked the door and they peered inside. Since no one had used the second story in years, a dense layer of dust shrouded the floor—except for one spot.

The pair discovered a distinct clean place in the dust, and marks across the floor where a chest of drawers had been dragged to the other side of the room—but no footprints.

"Isn't that strange?" Nancy remarked.

"Oh, don't worry about that." Cleo dismissed the strange occurrence with a wave of her hand. "That's just the ghost. But don't worry. It's a friendly ghost."

But Nancy's sons, Bruce and Shannon, did not find the incidence so out of the ordinary.

They'd both heard noises in the house since moving there earlier that winter.

When the house was dark and everyone was in bed for the night, Shannon would lie awake, listening for the disembodied spirit to begin its nightly rounds.

And then it would start.

Heel, toe.

Heel, toe.

The footsteps crossed the second story bedroom floor and then Shannon counted as they descended the seventeen stairs. Slowly, one by one. And then, without ever stepping on the first floor landing, the footsteps would pause, turn, and go back up the stairs.

Bruce also heard the strange footsteps, but he and Shannon were never frightened.

They both believed that the spirit who haunts the O'Neal house, is a benevolent one.

Although the family and Cleo didn't speculate as to whom the ghost might have been in life, it is safe to surmise that the spirit is connected with the O'Neal family.

The Governor Edward A O'Neal Home
468 N. Court Street, Florence, Alabama
Note the figure in the upstairs right window.

The house, at 468 North Court Street, was built in the 1840s, and belonged to members of the O'Neal family for over one-hundred and fifty years.

Edward Asbury O'Neal and his wife, Olivia Moore O'Neal, came to Florence from Huntsville in the 1840s. When Olivia saw the house under construction, she immediately fell in love with it.

Edward bought it for her in 1857.

Only a few years later, Olivia's lovely home was occupied by Federal troops when the Yankees came to Florence.

Edward was away, serving as a colonel in the 26th Alabama Regiment, and was later commissioned brigadier general for gallantry on the field under Hood's command. This left young Olivia and five of her children at the mercy of the occupation troops.

Edward Asbury O'Neal

When they left, the Yankees took everything that was not nailed down. They confiscated the O'Neals' personal valuables as well as the slaves, leaving the well-to-do O'Neals with nothing but the house.

It is difficult for us to imagine the horror and helplessness Olivia must have experienced seeing her expensive furnishings and things being trampled and seized by the Northern aggressors.

Still, this did not dampen her heroic spirit. During the war, she ministered to the sick and wounded Confederate soldiers and nursed injured relatives in her own home.

The O'Neals seem to have recovered quickly in the Reconstruction era. Edward was elected governor of Alabama and served two terms in the 1880s. His son, Emmet, later followed in his footsteps, making Edward and Emmet the first father and son governors in the history of Alabama.

Governor O'Neal died of a stroke on November 7, 1890, and Olivia passed away November 2, 1909, after suffering a heart attack. The house then passed into the hands of the O'Neals' daughter, Sydenham Moore O'Neal, and her husband, George Hiram Dudley. An unmarried daughter of Governor O'Neal, Julia, also lived in the house and died there in 1922.

Olivia Moore O'Neal

Sydenham was described by her mother as pretty and bright as a sunbeam. After her demise, her daughter, Mary Olivia Dudley inherited the O'Neal home.

Dressed in a gown of ivory duchess satin, with point lace appliqué and pearl trimmings, Mary Olivia Dudley married George Erwin Roulhac on January 8, 1913, at Trinity Episcopal Church in Florence.

George died only five years later at the age of 35 after contracting influenza.

Mary Olivia Roulhac returned to the O'Neal house with her son and she remained in the house until her death on August 11, 1970.

O'Neal Plot in the Florence Cemetery

In the 1990s, the house served as the Adrienne Ford Art Gallery. During that time, she rented the upstairs and the tenants complained about strange noises in the house at night.

For several years, the O'Neal home housed Alabama Outdoors.

One evening, after locking the business for the night, Karen, who managed Alabama Outdoors, heard the sound of footsteps upstairs. Her husband told her he'd checked, and there were no customers up there. Together, they went to investigate, but found no one.

During the summer of 2000, a young woman who'd been rollerblading on Court Street, stopped to rest on the porch. She heard a noise come from inside the house and when she turned and peered in one of the windows flanking the front door, she saw the transparent image of a woman with long blonde hair, dressed in an antiquated gown. With her hand resting on the banister, the ghostly lady gracefully glided down the stairs, seemingly unaware she was being watched. She stopped and looked out the window, then turned and walked back up again.

Could it be the governor's wife or perhaps one of his daughters, anxiously awaiting his return from the Civil War? Or maybe it is one of the O'Neals' descendants reenacting a haunting scene from her life. Perhaps it is Mary Olivia Dudley dressed in her ivory wedding gown, apprehensively descending the stairs to see if the carriage has arrived to take her to the church.

Students on the Haunted History of the Shoals Ghost Walk think they know who wanders the spacious rooms of the O'Neal home.

In 2012, a sixth grade field trip from Leoma Elementary had come to Florence to go on the ghost walk. At around noon on Halloween day, as the guide finished telling the story in front of the O'Neal home, she invited the students to wave good-bye to the O'Neals. One young man gestured to the upstairs window. "There's a lady up there now," he said.

The guide, their teachers, and sixty sixth graders stood at the edge of the street and looked up at the window. There stood the ethereal image of a woman clad in a long dress, with her hair done up in a bun.

If you happen to pass the lovely, historic home on North Court Street, you, too might politely offer a wave and say hello to Olivia O'Neal.

Could this be Mrs. O'Neal in the upstairs window of the O'Neal home?

THE GHOST OF THE WRIGHT-DOUGLASS HOUSE

The Kennedy-Douglass Center for the Arts is the arts cultural center for Florence. It houses the administrative office for coordination and promotion of cultural activities and is the home base and meeting place for various creative groups.

Fronting Tuscaloosa Street, it overlooks Wilson Park in the heart of downtown Florence. The Center is made up of three buildings - the brick Kennedy-Douglass house, the frame Wright-Douglass house, and the brick two-story carriage house.

The Kennedy-Douglass property was acquired in 1899, by Rebecca Jane Williams Douglass, the grandmother of Hiram Kennedy Douglass. The present Kennedy-Douglass house was constructed in 1936. The Wright-Douglass house was built in 1904, on the corner lot of Wood Avenue and Tuscaloosa Street by Elbert Bascome Wright.

In the 1980s, the Wright-Douglass house was renovated as an extension of the Kennedy Douglass Center for the Arts. It is used for many local arts events such as an annual sculpture display, as well as being the headquarters for the W.C. Handy festival. Piano recitals and artist receptions are frequently held there.

Therefore, it is surprising that a house with so much activity is home to a restless spirit.

Sometime in the late 1950s, Jewell and Elbert Darby purchased the house in downtown Florence. Before they moved in, Jewell's niece, Linda, recalled driving by with her parents one evening to get a look at the house. Linda remarked that a light was shining from an upstairs window. When her parents told her aunt about the light, Jewell found that strange. The utilities had not yet been turned on.

This was only the first unexplainable occurrence Jewell and Elbert would experience.

Linda's parents helped out on moving day and after a long day of exhausting work, the extended family collapsed in the living room to rest. That's when they heard the sound of the front door open followed by footsteps on the hardwood floor in the foyer.

When Elbert went to see who had dropped by for a visit, he was mystified to find no one there.

That same day, the children decided to play a game of hide and seek and some of them decided to hide in the bathtub. They did not stay hidden long.

The tortured sound of disembodied moaning drifted through the pipes, frightening the children out of their hiding place.

Both during the day and at night, Jewell heard the front door open and close but there was never anyone in the foyer.

Once, while she was in the kitchen, she heard the basement door open and close and heard footsteps descending the stairs. Knowing she was alone in the house, Jewell checked and found no one there.

One night, after they had gone to bed, they heard what sounded like a chair being tossed to the hallway floor from the upstairs but upon investigation, they found no explanation.

The noises were frightening enough but one night, Elbert witnessed something that changed his life.

He had retired early in the downstairs bedroom, and through the open door, he watched in horror as a mass of ectoplasmic energy collected at the top of the stairs. It floated down the stairs and came into the bedroom. Elbert lay there, frozen with terror. As the entity circled the bed, it took the form of a woman. She peeled back the covers on the other side of the bed and crawled in alongside Elbert.

Elbert passed out and when he finally regained consciousness, nauseated and terrified, he scrambled out of the bed and rushed into the living room where Jewell sat reading.

Without even giving her a chance to grab her robe, he ushered her out the door and into the car. He ran every red light on Wood Avenue as he sped to Linda's parents' house.

Linda recalled how his hands trembled as he drank his coffee the next morning and recounted the story to relatives. Elbert was so frightened, in fact, that he refused to ever go back in the house—not even to get his furniture.

But who was the entity Elbert observed? No one seems to know.

Sometime during the history of the Wright-Douglass house, it served as a boarding house.

Long-time KD employees were surprised to hear the house was haunted, though Mary Nicely, whose office is in the Wright-Douglass house, admitted to hearing the front door open one time when she was alone in the house at night. But when she went to check, no one was there.

Perhaps the ghost is proud of the many cultural activities the Center hosts and is quiet so as not to frighten anyone else. Or perhaps it is because the Kennedy-Douglass Center for the Arts is so replete with artistic activity, no one notices the ghost anymore.

THE HAUNTING OF BELLE MONT MANSION

Dr. Alexander Mitchell walked through the empty bedrooms on the west side of his recently built Jeffersonian style home which he and his daughters had named Belle Mont. His footsteps resounded on the white washed, heart of pine floors.

"Papa."

He whirled around, certain he had heard a voice.

But, sadly, there was nothing.

His heart wrenched as his gaze found the vacant little bed where his daughters, Sarah and Eliza, had once slept. The memories here were too raw, too painful. He closed the door and traced the design of the double witches cross with his fingertips—the pattern which was supposed to keep evil spirits out.

What had gone wrong here?

Dr. Mitchell shook his head and walked through the parlor, and then out onto the front portico of Belle Mont Mansion. But as he gazed down the hill, he took no joy or pride in his 1680 acre plantation.

With a heavy sigh, he leaned against one of the marbleized square columns and looked out over the white bolls of cotton which blanketed the ground all the way to the horizon.

With its vast expanse of cotton and corn fields Belle Mont was the grandest plantation south of the Tennessee River. The young trees Dr. Mitchell had imported from Prince's Nursery in New York, were maturing and bearing fruits of every kind. He had once dreamed of growing old here, of watching his two beautiful young daughters grow up in this paradise on earth.

But it was not to be.

He ran his hand through his dark hair, a sickening sense of helplessness washing over him. How could he remain here after the loss he had suffered?

First, five-year-old Sarah and now eight-year-old Eliza had contracted fever, their little lives slipping away within days of each other.

It was more than Alexander Mitchell could bear. He had already lost their mother and had left her buried in Virginia.

He had not even been allowed to bury his children together. Little Sarah was interred at Belle Mont and the authorities had made Alexander bury Eliza in Tuscumbia, fearing that even her corpse would spread the dreaded fever if the Mitchells brought her home.

Alexander swallowed hard, attempting to console himself by hoping they had all been reunited in death.

Unable to live in Belle Mont after the tragedy he had suffered there, Alexander Mitchell put his grand home and plantation up for sale. It was purchased by Isaac and Catherine Winston in 1833.

Belle Mont descended in the Winston family until the 1940s, when it was purchased by the Fennel family. For the earlier part of the twentieth century, Belle Mont was used to house tenant farmers and their families.

Many of these families would not stay long in the house.

Sightings of ghostly apparitions became frequent.

One late afternoon, as the setting sun cast long shadows across the double portico of Belle Mont, the wife of a tenant farmer was walking up the hill, tired from a hard summer day's work in the cotton fields. She brushed back her sweat drenched hair with the back of her hand and looked up, through the double line of ancient Cedar trees, at the weathered old mansion.

Belle Mont as it Looked in 1939

Through the open door, she noticed a woman and two little girls standing on the second story landing.

"Someone's in the house!" she screamed to her husband, who rushed to investigate.

He searched the vast rooms both downstairs and up but found no one.

Other tenant farmers have also reported seeing the woman and two children standing on the stairs and also on the front portico. They are always described as dressed in ordinary early nineteenth century attire.

The last recorded sighting of the Belle Mont ghosts was in 1968.

One tenant farmer actually claimed to have seen the ghostly family run down the stairs and out the front door. When the farmer went out to investigate, he discovered blood on the front porch. Chilled to the bone by the experience, he decided to wait until morning to clean up the blood.

Front Door of Belle Mont, 1939

Tenant Farmer on Back Porch of Belle Mont, 1939

Could the Mist on the Right Be One of Belle Mont's Ghosts?

But when he returned to the site the next day, there was no trace of the blood he had seen the night before.

Rumors of a brutal murder that took place in the house abounded but have never been confirmed.

Perhaps the wife of Alexander Mitchell and his two daughters have indeed found each other in the afterlife and haunted Belle Mont in search of Dr. Mitchell who had long since left.

Or maybe the ghosts are members of the Winston family who purchased the house from Mitchell in the early nineteenth century.

While the house was abandoned in 1970s, a descendant of Dr. Mitchell, Bo Lowery, was sitting on the upstairs portico with a friend enjoying the view when he and his companion heard the sound of heavy booted footsteps traversing the bedrooms downstairs. Alarmed that they might not be alone in the house, they went downstairs to investigate. No one was there.

That was not the only time Bo heard the heavy disembodied footsteps. Another evening when he was in the abandoned house, he heard the same sound coming from the ground floor.

Again, no one was in the house except Bo and a friend.

In the 1980s, Belle Mont, which had fallen into bad disrepair, was donated to the State of Alabama by the Fennel family and is currently being carefully restored by the Alabama Historical Commission.

The house is open for tours and is located near Tuscumbia, just off US 43 on Cook's Lane.

Belle Mont Has Been Restored and is Open For Historical Tours

The ghosts have yet to make reappearance and the tour guides are seldom bothered by their presence. But on windy, rainy days, mysterious footsteps are still sometimes heard traversing the ancient heart of pine floors.

YANKEE SPIRITS IN WESLEYAN HALL

The assertion that General William Tecumseh Sherman occupied Florence during the Civil War still sparks violent debate among Shoals historians. However, his supposed stay at Wesleyan Hall is linked to the legend of Turris Fidelis.

Most local folks know that Turris Fidelis is an award conferred annually by the University of North Alabama to a graduating senior for scholastic achievement and outstanding service to the university.

But Turris Fidelis is also a troubled spirit who walks the hallways of Wesleyan Hall when the moon is full.

There is some speculation as to whom Turris Fidelis was in life. Was he Colonel Wilson—a man whose son was kidnapped so Florence would not be burned by Sherman? Was he Wilson's son, Jeremiah, who drowned in Cypress Creek? Or was he General Sherman himself?

Perhaps all three ghosts haunt the Gothic Revival building. Completed in 1856, the three-storied structure is the mother building of the University of North Alabama. With its noble octagonal turrets rising like sentinels above the parapet line, Wesleyan has always been the pride of Florence.

Wesleyan Hall was designed by a Nashville native, Alolphus Heiman who served as a colonel during the Civil War. But it is widely rumored that one of his slaves was the actual architect of Wesleyan.

81

Postcard Depiction of Wesleyan Hall

Constructed by Zebulon Pike Morrison, Wesleyan served as the University for many years. The building housed classrooms, a library, and also served as the administration building for ten university presidents.

Wesleyan was also used as a headquarters for both the Confederate and Union armies. Federal troops stabled their horses on the ground floor and occupied President R.H. Rivers' office to spearhead their campaign. During renovation in the latter part of the twentieth century, remnants of a fire were discovered where a lantern used by Federal troops was believed to have ignited the first floor.

It was during this most turbulent period in Shoals history that the legend of Turris Fidelis was born.

According to clippings from the Birmingham News and a script for a play that was produced in Florence, called "History of State Teachers' College," General Sherman did, indeed, occupy Wesleyan Hall in November, 1863.

Often, during the Civil War, officers would bring along their teenage sons to serve as drummer boys. One of Sherman's colonels from Ohio, brought along his son, thirteen-year-old Jeremiah.

Young Jeremiah was the pet of the Union army.

Rumor has it that some of the townspeople may have kidnapped Jeremiah in order to use him to keep Sherman from burning Florence. The boy's disappearance naturally upset Colonel Wilson and enraged General Sherman.

General William T. Sherman, US

Sherman called in some of the town leaders and gave them an ultimatum: "Return the boy or I burn the town to ashes."

The boy was eventually returned unharmed but according to the legend, Colonel Wilson spent a tortured night in Wesleyan Hall fearing his son had been murdered. After his death, whenever, and wherever it occurred, Wilson's spirit has continued to return to Wesleyan Hall in hopes of finding the names of the men who kidnapped his son.

Another version of the story, as told to Dr. Gary Green by Mr. Noel Glasscock, asserts that Sherman occupied Wesleyan some time in either 1863 or 1864. Florence natives offered Sherman the use of Wesleyan in return for not burning and looting the city. The university library books were distributed among the townspeople to keep the Union forces from taking or burning them.

A Typical Union Drummer Boy

While Sherman was here, the weather was hot so young Jeremiah Wilson decided to take a swim in Cypress Creek near where the Wildwood Park Road bridge is now. He dove into the shallow water and either broke his neck or drowned. When his body was found, it was brought back to Wesleyan Hall where it lay in state until it could be shipped back to Ohio by train.

Dr. Green claims that on some nights, the stairs creak and moan as if unseen footsteps are ascending them. Sometimes, wet footprints can be seen leading from the door to the stairs.

Others have seen the ghostly image of a young boy clad in wet clothes, wandering the halls of Wesleyan at night.

Perhaps this is Jeremiah Wilson making the trek back from Cypress Creek where he met his untimely death.

Still, there are others who claim General Sherman is the ghost who haunts Wesleyan Hall.

In an article for the Flor-Ala, written in the 1950s, author, Joanne Harvey claims to have actually met and spoken with the ghost of General Sherman.

After hearing the legend, she went to Wesleyan alone on the night of the first full moon, and found a man bent over, in intent study, at a desk in the main office on the third floor. Too surprised to be frightened, she stood and stared. After a moment, he looked up and seemed as startled to see Joanne as she was to see him. He brushed back a shock of white hair and gazed at her as if to ascertain whether she was real or not. He smiled and rose, extending a cordial hand. "Forgive my rudeness," he said. "I wasn't expecting anyone and you caught me unawares. Do come in and sit down."

Joanne described his handshake as firm and his manner as one of accustomed authority.

Numb with astonishment, she sank into a chair drawn up beside his desk.

"Isn't is rather late for a young lady to be wandering alone in this deserted building?" he inquired in a gentlemanly fashion.

Joanne admitted she was a reporter for the Flor-Ala and told Sherman she was conducting research.

"I'm doing research work of a kind as well," he said and handed her an old piece of paper. "That is the ransom note of our drummer boy.

I'm trying to discover who kidnapped him and when I do——" he left the sentence hanging with threatening implication but then attempted an explanation. "You see, I am General Sherman, the man who occupied this building in 1863, the man who brought the stately and proud columns of the South tumbling down."

After allowing Joanne to absorb the impact of this statement, he rose and strode to the window, his hands clasped behind his back. "War is an ugly thing—a horrible thing. Death and destruction are part of it and have to be accepted as inevitable and unavoidable. But there was no excuse for the kidnapping of my drummer boy. The citizens of your town were so concerned that I might burn their university that they threatened to hang my boy. That is why Florence was spared my scorched earth policy. I could not risk my drummer boy's life." Then he turned, anger smoldering in his steel gray eyes. "They would have killed an innocent child for a few pieces of property."

Wesleyan Hall Today

Joanne did not argue. Instead, she made a hasty excuse for leaving.

As she left, Sherman called politely after her, "I hope I've been of some assistance to you. Please come again. I've enjoyed your company."

Perhaps all three ghosts traverse Wesleyan's ancient floors when the moon is full. Perhaps the ruthlessness of those turbulent years has left its ghastly impression in Wesleyan Hall, as a gruesome reminder of the destruction fear and hatred can render.

A HAINT IN THE GUY HOME

"Do you believe in haunts?" Lucy Abbot asked earnestly.

John Vandiver and his wife, Rosemary, exchanged glances.

John had always been skeptical about the existence of ghosts but after what had happened recently in his 1822 Colbert County home, he was a little more than curious as to what Lucy Abbot had to say.

Lucy's ancestors had once been tenant farmers who lived in the Guy home. She told the Vandivers what a wonderful man her father had been and how he had made sure his children had received a good education and that, although her family had not had much money, Lucy's father always tried to provide as best he could for his family.

Lucy's dark brown eyes grew wide as she continued telling the story of her childhood.

Growing up as the daughter of a tenant farmer in rural Alabama was not unusual for the times. But Lucy saw how hard her daddy worked and how they struggled to make ends meet.

She knew the history of the Guy home. It was old, built in 1822. It had been standing during the Civil War and Lucy had heard stories about how families had buried their valuables so the Yankee soldiers would not steal them. The Guy Home itself had been looted several times.

Stories were told that the Guy family had buried their gold under the house. She just knew it was true. And if she could find it, all her family's problems would be solved.

Lucy had heard footsteps in the house that didn't belong to any living person. She had also felt the chilling presence of some unseen entity.

And this is when Lucy developed her plan.

She would ask the Guy home's haunt if it could help her.

She began to talk to the ghost, begging it to tell her if there were any valuables buried near the house.

Her parents only chuckled when Lucy told them of her plan, but, undaunted, she continued to make her appeals.

And then one night, she felt a hand on her shoulder. "Lucy, wake up. Lucy."

A woman's voice roused her from her sleep and Lucy turned over to find the transparent image of a woman. Dressed all in black, and with her hair pulled back into a chignon, the woman smiled benevolently at her.

"I've heard your request, Lucy. I want you to tell your Father to go under the house and dig near the fireplace. There he will find a jar filled with gold."

Lucy was in shock. She was so frightened she could not even scream. Instead, she yanked the quilts over her head and did not dare look out again until morning came.

She told her father what had happened and her parents told her she had been dreaming. They never looked for the ghost's gold.

The Vandivers, however, took Lucy's story a little more seriously.

Just prior to Lucy's visit, they had experienced strange things in their house.

One afternoon when John Vandiver was staining the floor in the foyer, he heard the door open and then slam closed. The sound of a man's heavy boots on the wood floor resounded through the entry way.

Alarmed that someone was ruining his freshly painted floor, he leaned into the hall, fully anticipating seeing someone.

But no one was there.

The Guy Home

And once, while Rosemary Vandiver was home alone washing dishes, she heard the unmistakable clomp, clomp, clomp of boots walking down the upstairs hallway.

Terrified that someone had broken in on her, she dashed out of the house and down the driveway to where she met John who was returning from work.

Breathlessly, she explained that there was someone in the house. John went in to investigate, and again, found no one there.

After Lucy told them her story, they went under the house and dug on one side of the fireplace. No gold was found and the house sits too close to the ground on the other side of the fireplace for any serious excavation to be done.

Often, the Vandivers would discover that a chair pulled out in the dining room, as if someone has been sitting in it. And sometimes, while watching television, they'd hear the front door open and the sound of footsteps passing through the foyer.

But no one is ever there.

No one they can see, that is.

A FRIENDLY SPIRIT IN RYAN PIANO COMPANY

From 1942 until it closed in 2008, Ryan Piano Company was at the center of the local arts scene. Located at 207 East Tennessee Street, it served as the ticket outlet for the Muscle Shoals Concert Association, as well as numerous other Shoals plays and concerts.

But the downtown Florence building had not always catered to music lovers.

During the 1920s and early 30s, a gambling and prostitution racket headquartered in the building. The kingpin, a man named Hood, was the black sheep of a very wealthy Florence family. His upstairs office was the site of several shady dealings.

Vast amounts of money changed hands illegally in the building and Hood soon became involved with the New Orleans mafia.

Sometime in the early 1930s, the Florence kingpin's misdeeds caught up with him and he found himself the intended target of a mafia hit-man.

He fled Florence, moved to Texas, and only returned in disguise. After he died, his cremated remains were brought back to Florence to be interred in the Florence cemetery.

During the 1940s, with the arrival of the Courtland air base, many of the houses of ill repute and gambling establishments, once operated by Hood and his cronies, were shut down.

It was during this time, when downtown buildings became readily available, the manager of Forbes Music Company, Jeddy Ryan, seized the opportunity and went into business for himself, selling stoves and refrigerators alongside pianos to make ends meet.

Through the hard work of Jeddy and his wife, Ruth Ryan, and later, Robert and Noel Beck, Ryan Piano Company changed the unsavory reputation of 207 East Tennessee Street and earned an esteemed place in Shoals history.

Advertisement Announcing the Opening of Ryan Piano Company's First Location on Seminary Street

When Robert Beck decided to retire in 2002, I purchased the business and building from him.

It wasn't long after I bought Ryan Piano Company that I began to realize there was a presence in the historic 1922 building.

I'd practically grown up in Ryan Piano, and remember buying my very first piano book, *Teaching Little Fingers To Play*, from Mrs. Ryan back in 1972.

A few years later, I began taking piano lessons at the store from George Murray. I found studying piano with a concert pianist intimidating enough, but even more daunting was the climb up the steep flight of stairs to the second floor then walking all the way down the creepy, narrow hall to George's studio.

An eager student, I always arrived early and therefore, would have to wait in the hall until George was finished with the lesson before mine. The padlocked double doors to a recital hall-turned storage room seemed to breathe in and out on windy days. Lights flickered on an off. And I always had the eerie feeling that I wasn't alone in that dreary corridor.

Naturally, when I bought the store, I was curious to know if Robert Beck had ever experienced anything strange at Ryan Piano. Robert quickly stated that he didn't believe in ghosts but sometimes the stairs creaked and there were other noises in the store. Noises he attributed to the age of the building.

On dreary days, the stairs creaked and moaned as if unseen presence slowly and deliberately ascended them. The door leading to the second floor opened and closed of its own accord, an occurrence that I found particularly eerie when my (then) two-year-old daughter, Belle, raced to the foot of the staircase to wave at someone I couldn't see.

Many times, the front door opened, setting off the bell that alerted me to a customer, but upon investigation, I found no one there.

Once, I even heard a note ring out from one of the grand pianos when I was alone in the building.

When we filmed a television commercial at the store, the lighting kept falling over and the camera experienced technical difficulties. The camera men told me this had never happened before and one of them asked me if we had a ghost. I gave him a sheepish nod and told him we thought the ghost was possibly Mrs. Ryan. He then politely asked her to stop her antics and the rest of the shoot went without incident.

When the camera men began to edit the footage they had taken, they heard a thin reedy woman's voice on the film where the camera had malfunctioned.

One of the women, who taught music lessons upstairs after George Murray died, claimed to have felt George's spirit in the hallway—and a different male presence on the stairs.

When I closed the business for the night, I often had the strange feeling that someone was walking me to the door. Even my oldest daughter asked me about the *white light* that traced my steps in the store.

The old building retained a distinct smell of coffee and cigarettes, and sometimes Clubman barber's talc.

The fragrance was so decidedly masculine, it made me rethink Ruth Ryan's spectral presence in the store.

One morning, while I was playing one of the grand pianos, I saw a lightning flash out of the corner of my eye. A loud *bang* came from my desk and I dashed to see if my computer had possibly exploded. I found nothing amiss. No breakers had been tripped. There was no explanation for the mysterious blast.

More than once, the fine hairs on my arms and the back of my neck stood on end, bristling with an energy I could only describe as the sensation of trying to touch two magnets together. Though, I was ever alert, I wasn't really frightened by the presence in Ryan Piano Company.

Shortly after I took possession of the building, I learned who was responsible for the footsteps on the stairs.

My former mother-in-law had taught piano at Ryan's in the late 1950s, and on February 5, 1957, as she entered the store to practice with the piano ensemble, she was shocked to discover Jeddy Ryan, dead. He'd suffered a fatal heart attack at his desk.

I began to wonder if Mr. Ryan was indeed the male spirit I'd sensed in the building.

Only days later, something happened that would change my life.

The store was quiet. I sat, working on the computer. No radio. No TV. I had jokingly chastised the ghosts for being too quiet earlier that morning, so I suppose I was due for a little surprise.

Then, without warning, I heard an emphatic *Hello!* in my left ear. Startled, I jumped out of my chair, thinking someone was in the store. Heart hammering, I searched every room, both upstairs and down, every dank closet, the elevator shaft and even under the desk. But there was no one. The unexpected voice so unnerved me, I called my mother and talked until my pulse returned to normal.

As I talked to her on the phone, my ear began to burn. I looked in the mirror and the tip of my ear appeared to have been blistered.

Early in 2002, a customer came in the store to pick up some piano books for her grandchildren. She told me, "There's a man on your stairs. He was standing beside you when I first came in and then he went up the stairs."

Belle stayed with me at the store many afternoons and like most curious two-year-olds, she enjoyed exploring—especially the dangerously steep stairs in the back of the building. One day, she started up the steps. I scolded her from my desk, but undaunted, she continued climbing. I marched back there, snatched her up in my arms, intent on firmly explaining why she should keep off the stairs. Before I could scold her, the door at the top of the staircase creaked open. I gaped in horror as loud, heavy footsteps came toward us.

And then, Belle giggled and started to wave. "Hi Uncle Jeddy," she greeted. My gaze darted from her to seemingly the empty stairwell. I saw no one. But Belle apparently had.

What I found most odd was the fact none of us had ever mentioned Mr. Ryan to Belle. And yet, she knew his name was Jeddy.

I became more and more comfortable with my ghostly companion. But though others, including my daughters and a handful of customers, had seen him, I still had not. Boldly, I stood, arms akimbo, and called out to the vacant building. "All right, Mr. Ryan," I told him. "Several others have seen you. I'm no longer afraid. I'm ready. Appear."

Scanning the store's interior, I waited. But nothing happened.

And yet, he granted my request, in an unexpected way, the very next day.

The following morning, I unlocked the door as usual, and strode quickly through the dark building to the back where I flipped on the breakers. There, on top of an old table the Ryan's had used as a gift wrapping station, lay an old photograph I'd never seen before. I recognized Mrs. Ryan, though she looked far younger than she'd been when I'd seen her in person, and sitting next to her, was a striking, black-haired man, wearing wire-framed glasses and a white shirt. As if he thought I needed further proof, the photograph had been placed on top of a little brown booklet.

Chills swept over me when I opened the booklet and discovered it was the guest registry from Jeddy Ryan's funeral.

Far Right, Ruth Ryan, Center, Jeddy Ryan

Shaking, I scanned the photograph into my computer and emailed it to Robert Beck, with one question: Who is the man in this photograph? Robert called moments later, wondering where I'd found the photograph of Ruth and Jeddy Ryan.

I eventually did see Jeddy—at my house.

While working on my home computer, I noticed someone out of the corner of my eye walk up the stairs and start down the hall toward my office. He was tall, wearing glasses, dark trousers, a white shirt, had the sleeves cuffed twice, and the top button undone. He jangled loose change in one pocket, and in his other hand, he held a cigarette. He appeared quite opaque, however, he seemed cast in muted tones, like a faded photograph. The sight of him seemed so normal, I didn't realize anything was out of the ordinary—until he vanished in the doorway to my room.

Jeddy Ryan With His Nephew

Now, I begin my ghost walk with his story. One night, after the tour, a man approached me. He was quite shaken as he recounted his experience in Ryan Piano Company.

Shortly before I purchased the building, Robert and Noel Beck hired a couple of men to throw away several boxes that had been stored upstairs. A black-haired man in glasses, a white shirt, and dark trousers, emerged from one of the rooms and told him to leave several of the boxes. Assuming it was Mr. Beck, the man left the boxes only to be asked by Noel why he hadn't taken them. "Mr. Beck told me to leave them," he explained.

Noel informed him Mr. Beck had not been in the store that day at all.

I opened a book, containing a photo of Mr. Ryan and several others. The man pointed to Jeddy's picture. "That's the fellow I saw, the one who told me to leave the boxes."

I credit Jeddy Ryan with inspiring me to write not only this collection of ghost stories, but my others as well, and of course, for being the catalyst of my Haunted History of the Shoals Ghost Walk Tour. And even for playing matchmaker between my husband and me.

I closed the business in 2008, but like to think Jeddy is still an honorary member of our family—even if he is a ghost.

THE RESTLESS SPIRITS OF ROCKY HALL CASTLE

Very little exists to mark the spot where an imposing antebellum mansion once stood, set back from a country lane, other than a long row of burly cedars and a pile of rubble at top of a knoll a few miles from the quiet town of Courtland. In its heyday, the mix of Greek Revival and Gothic Revival architecture made Rocky Hill one of the most unique and ostentatious plantation houses in North Alabama.

In the mid-1820s, James Edmonds Saunders, a young lawyer who'd attended the University of Georgia, married his sweetheart, Mary Frances Watkins, and moved to Courtland where he hung out a shingle and opened a law practice. Perhaps young James was attracted to the rich Tennessee River farmland by his father, Turner Saunders, who owned a grand plantation house known as Saunders Hall.

Son, James Saunders, soon made a name for himself as a lawyer. He purchased a large tract of land about four miles from Saunders Hall and he hired a French architect to draw up plans for the grandest mansion North Alabama would ever see.

Construction on Rocky Hill Castle began in 1858. Completion of the house was delayed by the onset of the Civil War in 1861, but for many years the stately mansion stood as a monument to James Saunders' wealth and achievements. No expense was spared in the building of the Greek Revival, two-story structure. Crowned by an observatory, inhabitants could view the undulating cotton fields all the way to Muscle Shoals, Alabama, and look out over all the valleys and hills in between.

Saunders Hall

Porticoes graced the front and rear of Rocky Hill and the interior of the home featured intricate mouldings and spacious rooms with soaring ceilings.

The most unique feature of Rocky Hill Castle, however, was the Gothic, crenellated tower that stood sentinel over the property many years after the house itself crumbled away.

During the turbulent war years, Rocky Hill Castle served as a Civil War hospital. Doubtless, soldiers on both sides died as result of either their wounds or disease. Many of these fallen warriors lay buried in the adjacent Saunders' family cemetery.

Saunders, who became a Confederate colonel, entertained many southern military leaders in the home. Confederate General Joe Wheeler was most assuredly a frequent guest at Rocky Hill Castle since he lived nearby at his Pond Spring Plantation. Staunch southerners, JLM Curry and General Pierre Beauregard also visited Rocky Hill.

After the war, Colonel Saunders was never able to reestablish his pre-war wealth despite many entrepreneurial efforts.

Rocky Hill Castle

He died in 1896, and Rocky Hill eventually ended up in the hands of James' grandson, Dr. Dudley Saunders.

Dr. Saunders' family purportedly abandoned the house in the 1920s due to the extensive paranormal activity that plagued them.

Legends of the hauntings stem from the construction of Rocky Hill. Apparently, the French architect presented a bill so enormous, James Saunders grew angry and refused to pay the Frenchman. Uncompensated for his work, the architect left, but only after leveling a curse on the mansion and its "thieving master."

The hapless architect died shortly following his departure, cursing Rocky Hill. Soon afterward, inexplicable things began happening at the mansion.

Noises drifted up from the cellar as if someone were hammering but upon investigation, no *visible* culprit could be found. This activity continued as long as the Saunders family inhabited the house.

Whispers flourished that the Saunders were involved in an illicit slave trade. Some believed that a tunnel ran from the cellar of Rocky Hill all the way out to the Tennessee River. Slaves were allegedly transported down the river on barges, brought through the tunnel and forced to work in the vast Saunders cotton fields.

The Interior of Rocky Hill Castle
Note the Ghostly Face in the Upper Right Hand Corner

But the Frenchman wasn't the only ghost lurking on the grounds of Rocky Hill.

The most visible ghost at Rocky Hill is undoubtedly *The Blue Lady*.

During the Civil War, the tower was used to hide the family valuables, and also to conceal Confederates on the run from Union forces. Two unnamed southern soldiers died as a result of wounds in the tower. After they were buried in the Saunders family cemetery, a young woman, always seen dressed in blue, began to appear both inside and outside the house.

Mrs. Saunders encountered the young woman in blue on the

stairs of the house, and once, James Saunders saw the lovely, albeit terrifying, apparition in the wine cellar. That was the last time Saunders ever visited the wine cellar.

A Ghostly Image Inside Rocky Hill Castle

The Saunders family believed the blue lady was the sweetheart of one of the Civil War soldiers who'd died in the tower, and that her spirit had come in search of her lost lover.

In the 1920s, Mrs. Thomas Saunders, the wife of James Saunders' descendant, was preparing for her bath when she felt the eerie sensation of a presence in the room with her.

"Speak up!" she ordered the mischievous spirit.

She hadn't expected a reply, but she certainly received one.

"Do not be doubting, for I am truly here," a disembodied voice stated.

The Saunders family immediately packed their belongings and fled from the house.

Two Courtland businessmen purchased the property and allowed tenant farmers to inhabit the once grand house until the 1940s. After that time, vandals looted the Saunders family furnishings, pitted the grounds with holes they dug in search of buried valuables, and littered the interior of the house with graffiti.

Passersby made claims of hearing phantom piano music emanating from the once majestic parlor. Others reported seeing the ghostly image of the blue lady searching the grounds for her lost love.

The Tower Where the Blue Lady Searches for Her Lost Love

All that remains of the formerly grand antebellum home is remnants of the foundation and packed Alabama clay where the house and tower once stood. And of course, the legend of an angry architect whose curse destroyed James Saunders' fortune and Rocky Hill Castle in the end.

HAUNTED HISTORY OF THE SHOALS GHOST WALK TOUR

A spine chilling night awaits you in the company of a masterful storyteller who will entertain you with tales steeped in legend, folklore, and truth.

As twilight creeps over the homes and hidden courtyards of historic downtown Florence, prepare yourself to witness the mysterious and inexplicable.

Each year, during the week of Halloween, Debra conducts the Haunted History of the Shoals Ghost Walk Tour.

Souls depart at 7:30 pm, from Wilson Park in Historic Downtown Florence.

Tours last 90 minutes and cover approximately 1 mile.

Reservations are not required.

Visit www.FlorenceGhostWalk for more information, or to contact Debra.

Other Northwest Alabama Haunted Attractions:

Arx Mortis Haunted House

4051 Hwy. 72

Killen, AL 35645

WHERE DEBRA'S OTHER BOOKS CAN BE FOUND

Florence / Lauderdale Tourism
200 Jim Spain Drive
Florence, Alabama 35630
(256) 740-4141

Cold Water Bookstore
101 W. Sixth St
Tuscumbia, Alabama
(256) 381-2525

Ye Ole General Store
219 N Seminary St
Florence, Alabama 35630
(256) 764-0601

Lawrence County Archives
2588 Hwy 43 S
Leoma, TN 38468
(931) 852-4091

www.Amazon.com

ABOUT THE AUTHOR

DEBRA GLASS is the author of more than thirty five books. Since childhood she has been fascinated by things that go bump in the night. While writing True Shoals Ghost Stories Vol. 1, she realized many of the hauntings occurred in her hometown of Florence, Alabama, and decided to start a ghost walk tour. Since its beginnings in 2002, the Haunted History of the Shoals Ghost Walk Tour has become a perennial favorite during the Halloween season.

Debra lives in Alabama with her family, two smart-alec ghosts, and a glaring of diabolical black cats.

Other folklore collections by Debra Glass include:

True Shoals Ghost Stories Vol. 2

True Shoals Ghost Stories Vol. 3

Skeletons on Campus – True Ghost Stories of Alabama Colleges and Universities

Skeletons of the Civil War – True Ghost Stories of the Army of Tennessee

Haunted Mansions in the Heart of Dixie

Young Adult Paranormal Romance

Eternal

Debra conducts the Haunted History of the Shoals Ghost Walk Tour annually during the week of Halloween. For more information about Debra, her books, and her tour, check out her website: www.FlorenceGhostWalk.com

Made in the USA
Columbia, SC
16 June 2024

36693924R00067